For my father

www.mascotbooks.com

Walking A&P: A Vietnam War Memoir

For more information, please contact:
Mascot Books
620 Herndon Parkway, Suite 320
Herndon, VA 20170
info@mascotbooks.com

Library of Congress Control Number: 2018900799

CPSIA Code: PBANG0618A
ISBN-13: 978-1-68401-719-5

Printed in the United States

WALKING A&P

a vietnam war memoir

For Erin,
I hope you enjoy the book!
— Karol

KAROL NIELSEN

COMMISSION

Lincoln, Nebraska, 1941. My grandparents were at The Mug, a root beer stand that looked like a giant mug, when my grandmother said, "It's time." My father was born fifteen minutes after they reached the hospital. They named him Alan, but his father called him Bud.

My father played Cowboys and Indians in his backyard with his friend Dave. One boy had a bow and arrow, the other had a BB gun and took cover behind the wood pile. Sometimes they played Flaming Arrow. That meant tying a cloth around an arrowhead, setting it on fire, and shooting it into the air at night. The game ended when one stuck in the assistant district attorney's roof.

He also played games with his older brother, Russ. My father had found an old magneto from a Ford Model T but didn't know what it was, so his brother said, "Here, let me show you." Russ wired him up and turned on the power. The next time Dave came over, my father wired him up and turned on the power, too.

He went hunting with his father and mother. She spotted the birds in the field, and my father and my grandfather would shoot once the birds took flight. My father usually got a bird in one shot. He collected pheasant feathers and sewed pins onto the ends. He and his friends tossed them at each other. He also hunted rabbit and tanned the hides. He made mittens and a hat.

My father wasn't a wild man; he was clearheaded. His friend Donny used to drive drunk and speed along straight, flat Nebraska roads. My father would turn off the ignition as Donny drove, and when the car slowed to fifty, he turned it back on. He wasn't a square, but he knew where the line was and tried to keep his friends from crossing it, the way he did with his men in Vietnam.

My father was top of his Reserve Officers' Training Corps class at the University of Nebraska, serving as the commandant for the ROTC program on campus and leading all its parades. He studied chemical engineering at the university, because his brother was an engineer and his mother said that engineers made a lot of money, but my father liked leading better. In high school, his class wrote him in as a candidate for senior class president on the ballot, and he won without even campaigning. When he graduated from college, the army offered him a regular commission, like graduates of West Point.

IN COUNTRY

As soon as he landed in Vietnam, my father knew the military didn't have enough men on the ground to win the war. And the heat hit him like a hot smoky wind, making him sweat and sweat.

When he first arrived "in country," he didn't have a job for almost a week and he was lonely. He'd trained at Fort Sill, Oklahoma, the army artillery school, and finally he was assigned to an infantry company with the 101st Airborne Division as a forward observer, calling in fire when the company needed it.

The men were wary of my father, at first. The forward observer before him had lost his nerve during a firefight. He'd cowered behind a rice paddy dyke instead of calling in a fire mission, and as a result, the company suffered heavy casualties. My father was never one to crack under stress, but he had to prove himself to the men. They figured out fast that he always knew where they were and never got rattled in a firefight.

COOK

My father sorted his C-rations best to worst, trading the worst for his favorites, like beef spiced. His peanut butter and crackers always went to his radio operator, who only ate peanut butter and crackers. C's came in a big pack containing three meals a day for four days. My mother would send him popcorn, bouillon, and sweetened Kool-Aid in strawberry, grape, and lemon-lime flavors. He liked the lemon-lime best, because it took away the taste of the rice paddy water, made potable with halazone.

He'd cook his C's with bouillon, Vietnamese hot sauce (extra spicy), and rice. One of the meals came with a can of Velveeta cheese and a roll in a can, and he invented a way to make a grilled cheese sandwich inside the can. He cut the roll in half, added cheese, and put it back in the can. He then put the can inside the C-ration box and lit the box on fire—voilà! A perfect grilled cheese sandwich. Everyone envied his dishes.

My father started cooking when he was a boy. My grandmother asked him to peel the potatoes and set them to boil by the time she got home. She worked as a secretary in the capitol building in downtown Lincoln. He was her helper around the house.

Besides cooking, my father spit shined his family's shoes and did laundry. His family had a washing machine with a hand-crank wringer and two wash tubs, the first for rinsing and the second for bluing. (The process added a trace of blue dye to improve the appearance of fabric.) They hung the laundry on a clothesline. His sister, Susie, used to do the chores, but she married young and left home while my father was still a boy. His brother, Russ, was never asked to help. Russ was the brain, and my father had to cook him breakfast. Eggs. My father hated eggs, so he would make pancakes or cinnamon toast for himself instead.

My father had an instinct about how to cook, and when he didn't know how for sure, he'd experiment. In high school, he went to Valentino's Pizza, where the specialty was hamburger pizza. He made it at home with Chef Boyardee pizza mix. He added ground hamburger to the topping, but the crust turned out mushy and there wasn't enough cheese. The next time he tried it, he added a little more water to the crust mix and used an extra can of parmesan cheese. It came out perfectly.

His mother had set menus: chuck roast or fried round steak with boiled potatoes most nights, fried spam or cold canned salmon the other nights, and fried chicken on the weekends. He liked the spam—fried, it was almost like Canadian bacon—but he couldn't stand the canned salmon. On those nights, he'd warm a whole can of spinach for himself and douse it with vinegar. His mother never made him eat anything he didn't like.

This was nothing like his father's family, Danish immigrants who didn't indulge their children. His grandfather once accidentally substituted salt for sugar in pancakes, but still made his children eat them. My great grandfather left Denmark as a young man, settling in Iowa with his wife, Karolina—my namesake who would die in a tornado. He worked for the railroad, unloading coal cars by hand. It was brutal, relentless work that gave him a hernia. He died in his forties. My grandfather had to drop out of the eighth grade to support his mother and two younger sisters. He worked as a hod carrier for bricklayers, then as a clerk for the railroad after World War I because he was good with figures.

My father was a picky eater, even at his mother-in-law's house. "Scrambled eggs for dinner?" he asked my grandmother, a glamorous woman who had danced with the Radio City Rockettes. He took a sip of iced tea to clear his palate and grimaced: "There's sugar in this iced tea!" But he liked the venison and standing rib roast that my grandmother cooked. My grandfather hunted and raised cattle outside Lincoln.

My mother came from the wealthier part of town, but her father was a tough man. I liked him, though. He was a storyteller, a speed reader, a Golden Gloves boxer, and World War II hump pilot who flew cargo missions over the Himalayas from India to China.

Despite all his cooking, my father got so skinny in Vietnam that his Adam's apple became a big knot on his neck. He lost weight because of the heat and the constant movement with a heavy pack on his back. My father was so fit and light that he ran five miles in combat boots to buy a geisha doll for me and caught the Korean post exchange right before it closed. It was for my first birthday.

GRANDMOTHER

My father's mother didn't always believe that he would be as big a success as his brother. She often compared their abilities: my father was smart, but Russ was brilliant. She told my father in a letter he received while serving in Vietnam that she thought he'd only make it to the rank of major in the army. Promotions were almost automatic to that rank for career officers.

I don't know why she didn't think more of my father, but he knew she was wrong. If he'd wanted a career in the army, he knew he could go higher than major. But he figured out pretty quickly that he didn't want a career in the army; he didn't like the politics. He planned to leave the army, then earn an MBA and become a businessman.

GRANDFATHER

My grandfather was a clerk in the army during World War I. He encouraged my father to learn to type so that he could avoid combat, but my father wanted to be a soldier. He didn't know what his father thought when he joined ROTC; my grandfather didn't say. He didn't talk much, only when he had something to say.

My father's father was old enough to be my father's grandfather, and he was a gentle man who never raised his voice. Nobody shouted in my father's house. (Not like my mother's house where they got into it.) My father came from quiet, hard-working people.

My grandfather retired before my father finished high school. His brother and sister had already left home. My grandfather would get up at 3:00 a.m. to make coffee, play records, sing, and would be asleep on the couch by the time my father got up for school. Doctors thought he was depressed, so they gave him shock treatments. He died before the Vietnam War was over.

LETTERS

My father wrote letters every day. Some were just for my mother, others were for my mother, my brother, and me. The other men thought this was a little funny, like his cooking. They also got a kick out of his Bible lessons.

Most of the other men were unmarried teenagers, high-school-age kids out there fighting a war. Whenever he showed slides of his tour, he would choke up once he saw a skinny young man without a shirt, stretched out on the hood of a jeep. My father used to say that it's the young men who have no fear. They don't know about consequences yet. They think they are invincible.

In Vietnam, he tried to keep his men alive and keep them from doing anything they would regret later. He set a good example. He didn't drink or smoke or go after women. He treated his men with respect, and they respected him, too.

BURN

My father scrubbed his fatigues with Lifebuoy soap in a stream. While he did the wash, he wore his boxer shorts, like a kid in the backyard near the swimming hole.

He lounged in a chair, unprotected, as the desert-hot sun seared his skin. (The army didn't supply sunblock in rations; besides, it was so hot he would have sweat it off.) His back blistered, and the shoulder straps of his backpack tore away layers of skin.

While his back healed, his radio operator, Virgil, carried half of his supplies, cutting the weight from about 80 to 40 pounds. Virgil wasn't a tall man, but he was solid as a linebacker. He was part Mexican and part Native American with a wry, friendly smile. His mother sent him deer jerky, and he shared it with my father.

WALKING A&P

My father traded his small, low-slung army-issue backpack for a much larger long-range reconnaissance patrol pack with an internal frame. He could now carry extra ammunition and canteens of water, halazone tablets, C-rations, and all the things he had begun to collect—Vietnamese hot sauce, chicken and beef bouillon, onions, rice, popcorn, beef jerky, cashews, Kool-Aid, and once even a couple of Cokes. He was a grocery store on foot, and his men called him the Walking A&P. They would place bets on who'd get his pack if he got scuffed.

One day, my father's company stopped for a rest on the Ho Chi Minh trail. It was hot, hundred-degrees hot, and the air was thick with humidity. They were on a steep mountainside trail. All the men were exhausted, sweating profusely, lying down anywhere they could.

This was the moment my father and Virgil had been waiting for. They got out two Cokes, popped the caps off. Everyone within earshot lifted their heads and watched as they slugged them down. When they finished, they both belched loudly, and said, "Let's have another." The men nearby jumped up and looked like they were going to attack. My father and Virgil laughed at having pulled off their well-planned joke.

VIET CONG

Up in the Central Highlands, the forest was a thick canopy with heavy undergrowth that was almost impossible to walk through if you weren't on a trail. Wait-a-minute thorn bushes grabbed people, forcing them to stop and free themselves. Even the animals used the trails.

At night, it was so dark that you couldn't see your own hand in front of your face. At first, my father was afraid of the dark, but he quickly realized that if he couldn't see the Viet Cong, they couldn't see him. The dark became his friend, the darker the better.

The VC was made up of men and women and sometimes children. Their uniform looked like black pajamas. My father's company commander wore black pajamas at night, for cover. The women fought just like the men, and the first severely wounded soldier my father saw was a female VC. She was pretty, petite, and young, but it was always hard to tell someone's age because the Vietnamese seemed to age more slowly.

This was my father's first patrol. The company had been following the trail along a riverbed most of the night, and before dawn, they rounded a bend and met with heavy gunfire coming from a small village on the banks of the river.

The injured woman was lying in the trail with an AK-47 by her side. She was near a hamlet of thatched-roof homes, and she was probably left behind as a guard, to fend off the Americans. The others were already running up the hill between ridges.

Her leg, nearly shot off, bent unnaturally at the knee. She looked up at my father, her mouth opening and closing without saying anything, as if gasping for breath or final words. Nothing could have been done for her. He had to call in artillery to push back the VC, and when the firefight was over, it was clear that the young girl was dead.

THE GOOD BOOK

Gunfire broke out as my father was flown in a helicopter to a new position. He felt bullets hitting the helicopter before it went down. The helicopter was a mangled mess, but it didn't catch fire. Only the cockpit bubble remained intact, and the pilot and copilot were still strapped in their seats lying on their backs. The men rescued the pilot and the copilot from the helicopter. Somehow, the other men had escaped from the helicopter unhurt and were scattered, like sheep on a green hillside.

They had no idea where they were. It was my father's job to figure out their position and call it in. My father lifted his head to look at the surrounding terrain. He could see North Vietnamese army (NVA) soldiers about a hundred yards above them on the hilltop. A bullet knocked his head back as it grazed his helmet. He ducked down and studied his maps, realizing that the pilot had landed on the wrong side of the hill. They had flown off course.

Once he knew where he was, he called in tactical air support and artillery fire from the battery about four miles away. They later realized that if the pilots had landed where they were supposed to, they would have been landing right in the middle of an ambush. Going down on the wrong side of the hill protected the men because it caught the NVA off guard.

After my father's infantry company secured the hilltop where the helicopter had crashed, they collected all the enemy dead and wounded. My father found a wallet in the fatigue pocket of one of the dead NVA soldiers. It contained a photo of his wife and two children, which reminded my father of his family. As he looked at the photo, my father realized this soldier was just doing his job, and under different circumstances they might have been friends.

My father read the Bible and Christian Science textbook every day. He carried his small leather books in plastic bags, tucked in his chest pockets. They were books that my mother's uncle had carried during World War II.

The men ribbed him about it, as if he were a Boy Scout or a pastor—a real square. Before the mission that day, he was reading the Bible. A platoon leader came over and said, "Okay, put that away. It's time to go." After the mission, the men all said, "Keep reading the Good Book."

ORDERS

Once in a while, some big battalion-level guy would fly out to the field and throw his weight around. Soon after my father replaced the forward observer who had cracked up and caused heavy friendly fire casualties, the infantry battalion executive officer arrived to step in after the company commander had been wounded. His job was to reestablish the company as a cohesive fighting unit. He was particularly intent on shaking up the new replacement forward observer, my father.

The first night, he ordered my father to be sure that the harassment and interdiction fire around the company was "in tight." (H&I fire protected the platoon at night by placing intermittent fire about 50 to 100 meters outside the perimeter to stop the enemy from creeping up to attack.) My father said, "Yes, sir," and gave his artillery battery the firing instructions for that night.

The H&I fire was indeed tight. The artillery rounds exploded as they hit the treetops above the company's position, and shrapnel tinkled down through the leaves all night long. In the morning, the battalion executive officer came to my father and said, "Tonight you can move the H&I fire out a little."

Later that same day, while they were stopped for a lunch break, the battalion executive officer asked my father where he thought they were located on the map. My father pointed to the grid coordinate on the map where he thought they were. The battalion executive officer disagreed. They were near a small clearing that had a single tree in the middle. One squad was lounging around the tree eating their C-rations. The executive officer said, "Okay, if you think you know where we are, fire a smoke round at that tree."

My father said, "Sir, you'd better tell those men to move."

The battalion executive officer said, "Look, God damn it, just fire it."

"Yes, sir," my father replied and called in one round of smoke on the tree. The smoke round burst right above the tree, and the canisters of smoke encircled the tree. The men around the tree jumped up and scattered. The battalion executive officer didn't say anything. He just turned and glared at my father. He realized my father "knew his shit," and from then on, he never questioned him.

A firefight broke out one day in the jungle. The company had to hit the ground for protection from the intense small-arms fire. After the firefight began, the infantry battalion commander was circling overhead in his helicopter acting like a big shot and telling the company commander to attack the hill and get those "little sons of bitches."

The company commander wanted to respond, "Why don't you fly your ass down here and show us how it's done?" Since he knew that he couldn't say that, he said, "Sir, we're taking heavy fire and the only thing keeping me from getting closer to the ground is my shirt."

The battalion commander came back with, "What the hell are you saying?"

The company commander said, "Sir, you're breakin' up! I can't read you. Out!"

For several minutes the battalion commander kept calling, but the company commander didn't answer because he knew the battalion commander had no idea what was going on down on the ground.

JUNGLE CLOTHES

When my father landed in Vietnam, he had cotton fatigues, leather combat boots, and wool boot socks. Leather, cotton, and wool are not the best materials in a wet, tropical climate. Quick-drying materials that breathe were needed. While jungle fatigues and boots were available, the rear-area people responsible for administration, logistics, medical supplies, and other combat support functions were taking the first shipments. It was well into my father's tour before he got jungle boots and fatigues.

Vietnamese civilians coped with the climate by wearing what looked like silk pajamas and sandals with soles made from the treads of discarded tires. The Montagnards—indigenous peoples in the Central Highlands—usually went barefoot and only wore tire-soled sandals during the rainy season because their feet would become soft and could be easily cut. In the dry season, their calloused feet became their sandals, tougher than shoe leather. The men wore loincloths, and the women wore topless sarongs.

SHOWER

While my father was a forward observer with the infantry, he wore the same set of fatigues for several weeks as he trekked through jungle trails, walked through rivers, and waded through rice paddies. His clothes were ripped by the wait-a-minute thorn bushes in the jungle. Periodically, they would be flown to a field staging area where the army had set up showers.

The process was simple: take your clothes off and throw them away, enter the shower tent, take a shower and shave, walk out the other end, dry off, and put on a new set of fatigues. Then he was set for another month.

STARS

Base camp seemed like a four-star hotel to my father, after weeks in the field. He couldn't get used to it. The hot chow, the down time. Too much time to think. He missed my mother and my brother and me.

I was a baby when he left. He called me Tootsie in one of his letters home. He told my mother to feed me pulse so I'd grow, like the Bible story about Daniel, Hananiah, Mishael, and Azariah who ate pulse and water and were healthier than the boys who ate the king's food.

At night, he'd get lonely when he looked at the stars. He thought of my mother in hot pants. He didn't know why; she never wore hot pants, but he thought of her in them anyway. He dreamed of a place beyond the jungle and the war.

He'd never seen so many stars. The atmosphere was so clean that he could see constellations—crisp and clear polka dots. He could see the Big Dipper, the Little Dipper, Orion's Belt. He mapped the company's direction using the North Star. He knew the stars, like coordinates on a map.

GOOD LIFE

My father found a banana on a tree. That was rare. Most fruit trees and gardens had been picked bare. The Viet Cong mostly ate rice and cassava. Sometimes my father traded his C-rations for a South Vietnamese soldier's long-range reconnaissance meal: a plastic bag containing rice and dried fish. The Vietnamese carried cooked rice in long black boot socks. They usually had two or three of them hanging on their backpack. Often, they would eat a handful of the gummy rice, and sometimes they would add fish.

My father carried a pot tied to his backpack and learned to cook rice like the Vietnamese. He covered the pot with a lid and held it closed with a flexible, green twig. He cooked it until little holes dotted the rice, like the holes left by clams in the sand.

The other men always wanted what he'd made. Most only bothered to warm their can of C's. Some ate their rations cold. My father couldn't stand them cold or plain. A well-prepared C-ration dinner in the field made him feel like he had a good life.

He cooked even when he was filthy. He always joked, "After four days you don't get any dirtier." Back home, he was Mr. Clean, and my mother was messy. He told her that he read a Dear Abby post that said, if your wife or husband doesn't like to clean, then do it yourself.

DUCK HUNTING

My father's company caught duck in a rice paddy. They used their ponchos as nets to catch the birds, like fishing in a swamp. They looked forward to the duck, but the meat was gamey and tough. The mosquitos were bad and did a number on them.

They tried to give the duck to the Montagnards, but they didn't want it. It reminded my father of trying to give away ham and lima bean C's. "No got-damn good," the old man had said. He wore a loincloth and had flat, bare feet.

The Montagnards made good guides. They could hear subtle sounds and see far away. They could read the sun and the stars, like my father. He also counted steps. All day, day after day.

He marked his position step by step by step, cross-referencing with coordinates on his maps. He had to make sure that he knew exactly where they were at all times so that the artillery battery could fire support missions and not hit them.

My father never had a friendly fire incident, meaning he never accidentally called in fire on his own troops. This only happened if the guy calling in the fire didn't know exactly where he was. But my father was always prepared and always knew exactly where he was and where his troops were.

RAIN FOREST

My father saw tiger claw marks on a rubber tree and elephant dung on the dirt trail near the Cambodian border. But he never saw a tiger or an elephant, only monkeys, donkeys, water buffalos, ducks, and chickens.

It was summer, and it was wet in the rain forest. During the day, my father carried his air mattress and poncho liner rolled up in his poncho to keep them dry. My mother eventually sent him a rain suit, a life saver that kept him dry and warm. It dipped down to the high forties or low fifties Fahrenheit at night, and he had never felt colder.

My father would use monkey vine as rope and tie his poncho between two trees to make a hooch—a kind of hut. He used banana leaves at the ends to keep out the rain. He would blow up his air mattress, take off his wet clothes, and sleep in his poncho liner. He often slept naked so his clothes could dry out. Rainwater ran underneath him, and it was like sleeping in a stream bed.

My father would string his hooch so that rainwater funneled off the sides into his steel helmet. He poured the rainwater into three canteens and one jungle water pack, which could hold a gallon of water. The rainwater was good because he didn't have to put halazone tablets in it, but it gave him the runs.

At night, he wedged a flashlight with a red filter under his chin so that he could read the book my mother had sent him, *Old Jules*, about a crusty old homesteader. He wasn't kind, like my father. Usually there was no time to read, but he read whenever he could. My mother sent him a bunch of books, mostly about Nebraska. He liked them because they reminded him of his roots.

DESERT

Most of Vietnam is tropical with lots of rain, but some places are like the desert. Phan Thiet, a coastal town, is one of those places. My father's company was stuck there in the sand dunes for two days without water. A man can go without food but not water. A 250-gallon tank was finally helicoptered in.

The tank had been sitting on a tarmac baking in the sun. The water was so hot, they had to let it cool all night before they could drink it. Since there were no VC in the area, the company left this location after a couple of days.

On the way out, they spotted a boy on the roadside selling licorice soda pop. My father bought two bottles and chugged them down. They were ice cold and tasted delicious going down, but almost immediately he threw up. He still can't stand the smell of licorice. After Phan Thiet, he always carried at least seven quarts of water. He was never going to run out of water again.

HOT ZONES

My father wrote to my mother about hot zones but didn't tell her all the details. He kept it simple. He told her the numbers. That's how they counted progress in the war: numbers.

He told her things like the 173rd Airborne pushed the North Vietnamese army back across the Cambodian border; the 101st Airborne got into a fight with the Viet Cong, when two hundred were killed in action, more wounded; on patrol, they found a North Vietnamese camp with rice and cassava still cooking.

He deliberately left out any references to combat he was involved in. He knew my mother wanted to know where he was and what he was doing, but he didn't want her to be afraid. My mother said that the way he wrote his letters did help, but she still had a big knot in her stomach the whole year he was gone. She was terrified that he might not come back.

MALARIA AND
JUNGLE ROT

After Phan Thiet, the company moved to a staging area to wait for the next mission. Within the first few nights, my father became feverish and sick to his stomach. He didn't think too much of it and thought it would go away. But by about the third night, he was so feverish and ill that he was delirious and disoriented. The company medic looked at him and called for a medical evacuation because he was pretty sure that my father had malaria.

My father was taken to a field hospital in Cam Ranh Bay. He was put in a cold shower two or three times a day, and he took so many malaria pills that his ears rang and everything tasted like quinine. After a few days, he was finally well enough to get a medic to write a letter to my mother about the malaria, asking her to call a Christian Science practitioner for help. When my mother received the letter about a week later, she immediately placed the call. It was made about noon in Nebraska, which was about midnight in Vietnam. My father woke up about midnight that night and knew he was getting better. He felt almost normal.

Growing up, my father was a Lutheran and a choir boy. He told us about sneaking into the church kitchen after the service and sipping the wine leftover from communion. He also did it with Dave in his church, because they had communion on different Sundays. As a teenager, he was especially fond of his beer and carried a pack of Luckies rolled up in his white T-shirt sleeve. Now my mother's religion had become his own. Christian Scientists didn't drink or smoke or take medicine. But he'd taken the malaria pills because he could have been court-martialed if he hadn't taken them.

About a dozen men from his company also came down with malaria about the same time. Bug repellant was supplied to the men, but the joke was that at night the mosquitos would shake you to wake you up to put on more bug juice because they liked it. The men thought that the repellant didn't work, but it was a good fire starter.

When my father went to the hospital, he also had a bad case of jungle rot on his feet and ankles. They scrubbed it a couple of times a day with hydrogen peroxide, which turned into foaming bubbles. The rot soon cleared, but he still has faint scars around his ankles. He learned not to wear socks or underwear.

When my father was in the infirmary, he overheard two orderlies talking about how hard they had it. Long days of twelve hours, sometimes more. They had to work weekends. It was an injustice. They spoke as if they had the hardest jobs in the military—the hardest in the war. It was as if he wasn't even there.

He was so delirious that he could only listen to them. They have no idea what it's like in the field, he thought. Walking all day, seeing action, going days without water and a bath. He thought of the young man who'd stepped on a land mine, his leg blown off below the knee. The injured man radioed his SOS to my father and his radio operator. He was in agony, and there wasn't time to get to him. He was afraid to die. My father spoke to him until he died. It wasn't long.

After my father got better, he ventured out on the beach. He'd never seen such fine white sand. The bay had blue jellyfish, shaped like mushrooms. He played volleyball even though he didn't have the strength to jump. His red blood cell count was low, like my mother's before I was born. (She had to eat a lot of iron; fortunately, she liked liver).

The doctors wanted him to stay at Cam Rahn Bay for another two or three weeks and take medication to replenish his red blood cells, but my father felt that his place was back with his men. So he convinced the doctors that he would be fine and could go to his unit. They said okay. He went back to his unit and quickly recovered his strength.

MAIL

My mother sent letters and tapes to my father, trying to keep him involved in day-to-day family life, as if he were away on a long business trip. She told him about our lives—me biting my brother, the dog pooping on the ironing board, a broken refrigerator, car loan payments, dates for his graduate school entrance exams in Saigon.

My father spent the whole year planning his exit from the army, having my mother send away for MBA applications for schools in Washington, Colorado, Michigan—places he'd like to live. His older brother, who had a PhD and was a chemical engineer working in New York City, suggested Columbia University, but my father wasn't too impressed.

When my father first arrived in Vietnam, his mail was held up for weeks. My mother wrote a letter to her congressman, her senator, and even the president to complain about the mail service. It led to an investigation.

One day, my father's unit was in the field and had briefly stopped about noon to rest and eat, when a captain from the 101st Airborne helicoptered into the position. He stepped off the helicopter and said, "Is there a Lieutenant Nielsen here?"

My father said, "Yes, sir." He handed my father a packet of about fifty letters, about six weeks' worth of mail, and said, "Tell your wife you got your mail and not to write to the president again!" He got back on the helicopter and flew away.

BRASS

A big offensive mission was about to begin, and my father's battery was going to neutralize the landing zone where the infantry battalion was going to land. My father was now fire direction officer of the battery.

Just as he began to have the fire direction center prepare all the firing data and instructions, the artillery battalion executive officer flew into the battery and immediately went to the fire direction tent to ask questions, issue orders, and generally disrupt the flow of work my father was responsible for getting done.

After a few minutes of frustration, my father handed his graphical firing table (an instrument that looks like a slide rule) to the battalion executive officer, walked out of the fire direction center, went down to the stream at the edge of the fire base, and took a swim.

After the mission was complete, about an hour later, he returned to the fire direction center. As he walked in, the battalion executive officer said, "Where the hell have you been?"

My father said, "I thought you wanted to run the mission, so I just got out of your way and went for a swim." After a long silence, the battalion executive officer cracked a smile, handed my father the graphical firing table, walked out of the tent, got in his helicopter, and flew back to battalion headquarters.

After my father's battery had lifted into a new position, the infantry battalion executive officer flew in to inspect it. For the first couple of days in a new position, the men had to do a tremendous amount of work. They dug in and sandbagged each of the six gun positions as well as ammo bunkers and foxholes for more than 100 men. They also cleared elephant grass and cut or shot down trees in the line of fire.

My father walked the new position with this battalion executive officer who made a number of ignorant and petty comments, such as pointing out the messy appearance of the men's individual foxholes where they slept. My father, who had heard enough, said, "Sir, these men actually have to stay here tonight. They won't fly back to a bunk and clean sheets."

Like other run-ins with rear-area brass, often referred to as "rear-area motherfuckers," the battalion executive officer abruptly turned around, walked over to his helicopter, flew out of the position, and never returned. In confrontations like these, my father always said, "What are they gonna do, send me to Vietnam?"

BAIT

In Vietnam, the artillery was often used as bait. A battery would be airlifted into the center of what was believed to be a VC or NVA hot zone, hoping the enemy would attack the battery. Infantry units were queued up in nearby staging areas, ready to be flown in the moment the battery was attacked. This was made possible by the introduction of a new 105-mm howitzer—model M102.

It was brought into service at the beginning of the Vietnam War, and the 101st Airborne Division got it first. The older model—M101— was a mainstay weapon during World War II, when the artillery was generally behind the front lines and only fired forward. There are six guns in a battery, traditionally lined up in a row and all pointing in the same direction, but the M101 could only aim 45 degrees left or right of center. It could not easily be moved to fire in another direction because it was anchored into the ground, keeping the gun in place while firing. As a result, the old M101 howitzer could not be used to effectively protect the battery because it was too difficult and time-consuming to change the direction of fire. However, the new M102 howitzer could rapidly change direction of fire through a full 360 degrees.

With this 360-degree capability, a new formation called the star was adopted. In this set up, five guns were arranged in a star and one was placed in the center. When the guns were not engaged in a fire support mission (when all guns fired in the same direction), each gun at the five points of the star would be pointed outward from the center. The barrels of the five guns would be lowered level with the ground into the direct fire position. If the battery was attacked, each gun could quickly be fired outward, like a big shotgun, to defend the battery. At night, the barrel of the gun in the center would be elevated to almost vertical and was prepared to fire illuminating rounds.

At maximum range for a 105-mm howitzer, a 1-mil firing error would result in a 12-yard error on the ground. On the other hand, a one-degree error would result in a 225-yard error or two and a quarter football fields. There are 6,499 mils in a circle, equating to 360 degrees. A mil is approximately twenty times more accurate than a degree, which is why the artillery uses mils instead of degrees.

My father made his men practice their firing skills constantly, particularly for night missions. He knew that 1 mil could often be the difference between life or death for the infantry unit they were supporting. Artillery defensive fire was often within 50 yards of friendly forces.

WILSON

The big guns were fired regularly during the night. My father could sleep through howitzer fire, but the sound of small-arms fire woke him. Small-arms fire meant something was wrong. That's what he heard when the North Vietnamese crept up before dawn and took out the men in about a third of the foxholes protecting the perimeter. The battery was in a valley between two ridge lines beside the Song Ba River. Elephant grass surrounded the perimeter. A platoon of Americans was guarding the perimeter instead of South Vietnamese troops.

My father always slept with his M16 rifle right by his side. When he heard gunshots, he rolled off his cot as bullets ripped through his tent. Later, he saw that a bullet had sheared an 18-inch cut in his cot. He ran to the nearest gun pit. The crew was hiding in the gun's ammo bunker for protection. He yelled, "Get the hell out here and prepare to return direct fire!" He then ordered an illumination round from the center howitzer and an antipersonnel round from another gun.

He had not seen this particular site in daylight because he had come in after dark. He had to decide from sounds and muzzle flash where to point the gun to fire the antipersonnel round to stop the attack. He yelled, "Everyone get down, we're going to direct fire an A-P round!" He ordered the crew to fire the antipersonnel round, which was filled with about 5,000 flechettes. He could hear screams as the tiny darts pierced flesh, like a swarm of nails. Later, the men said it sounded like the NVA soldiers were cussing Ho Chi Minh.

It took about forty-five minutes to repel the attack and put the enemy into retreat. Once the perimeter was secured, my father began to check for casualties. His first stop was the fire direction tent, where he found his friend Wilson, lying on the ground, eyes open. He told him to hang on, thinking he was still alive. He called for the medic, but it was too late. Wilson was gone. "It was such a waste," my father always said.

It was a new position, and most of the men had worked until early morning setting up the battery, digging bunkers, filling sandbags, stacking them up. Wilson's commanding officer took pity and didn't make his men finish digging in. He let them sleep in the fire direction tent. Wilson calculated the firing data, including elevation and direction for the guns and the number of bags of propellant to hit the target. These days, this job would all be done on hand-held devices with GPS.

When the NVA hit the battery, Wilson was sleeping in the fire direction tent. They hit the fire direction center first because they thought it was the nerve center of the battery, believing it was in the back of the battery so the guns couldn't be turned on them. They didn't realize that the new howitzers could rapidly turn 360 degrees. Everything happened so fast that Wilson wouldn't have had time to try to defend himself.

My father and Wilson had worked closely together until my father had been promoted to executive officer of the battery and Wilson was no longer his direct report. Wilson was a hard case. He was an enlisted man with a bad attitude. He'd been court-martialed several times for disorderly conduct and demoted to the rank of private. He had been given to my father to either "shape him up or ship him out." Somehow Wilson and my father connected and he became a different man. He completely shaped up and even spoke of applying to Officer Candidate School when he got back to the United States.

My father wrote to my mother after he was awarded a Bronze Star with V for valor for his leadership. He told her he wasn't trying to be a hero; he was just doing his job. This was the first time in the nine months he'd been in Vietnam that he told my mother about a battle he had been in because he knew it would be in the newspaper.

TOP

My father's tent mate in the battery was Sgt. Richard Cromartie, the chief of firing battery. The men called him Chief of Smoke or Top. He was the top noncommissioned officer of the battery with about 80 of the 120 men in the battery reporting to him.

Top was a small, quiet man with a big presence. The men never messed with him because he was tough. They weren't afraid of him, though. They respected him and so did my father. Top and my father worked more as partners than as commanding officer and subordinate. They would check on each other to make sure nothing was overlooked. They shared family values, rice, and responsibility for the men.

When the battery moved to a new firing position, Top always came in on the first lift with the advance party. His job was to quickly assess the new position before the guns started to arrive, clear the area of tall brush and grass, set up two of the six guns for fire support, shoot down any trees that were blocking lines of fire, then strategically place the remaining four guns as they each arrived. He also made sure that the men were digging in and sandbagging every gun position, ammunition dump, foxhole, and tent. My father knew that everything would be exactly right by the time he got to the new position.

When the battery was ambushed, both my father and Top instinctively knew what to do. While my father went to the closest gun to order the crew to fire flechettes into the middle of the main attack, Top went to the center gun to get the crew to fire illumination rounds. He had them fire rounds until dawn broke. He also commanded the other four guns to help repel the attack and keep the unpenetrated parts of the perimeter secure. Like my father, Top was awarded a Bronze Star with V for valor for his actions.

LEADER

My father wanted the men to know that he wasn't the kind of leader who would ever ask them to do anything that he wasn't willing to do. He used to walk the perimeter every night, stopping at every foxhole, so the men knew he wasn't afraid to be out there with them.

When American troops were on the perimeter, my father would call on the field telephone, which was in each foxhole. He'd crank the telephone to call, and all the phones would ring. He would tell whomever answered that he'd be coming out to the perimeter. He didn't want them to get spooked and accidentally shoot him. Sometimes Vietnamese guarded the perimeter, so instead of a phone call, he would shine his red flashlight on his face and whistle while he walked, so they would see and hear him coming.

C'MON BABA

When the men had been out on operations for more than a month, they all needed haircuts. On one occasion, the battery commander ordered the ammo sergeant, Sgt. Smart, to get on the next resupply helicopter back to base camp, go to the nearby village, and bring a couple of barbers back to the battery. Sgt. Smart, a giant of a man, went into a barbershop in the village, grabbed two of the barbers by their shirt collars, and said, "C'mon, baba."

The barbers had no idea what was happening. Sgt. Smart loaded them on the afternoon resupply helicopter and flew back to the battery, landing about nightfall. He put them in the ammo bunker for shelter for the night. They huddled in the corner, not knowing what was going to happen to them in the morning.

The next morning, they were told to start cutting hair, and for the next two days they gave about 120 haircuts. Each man paid them a dollar. On the morning of the third day, Sgt. Smart grabbed them again to put them back on the helicopter going back to base camp and home. They were all smiles and didn't want to go. They'd never made so much money before, and they wanted to stay.

LIVER

Once in a great while, hot chow would be flown out to a firing position. It was cooked several hours beforehand, then sealed in Mermite cans to keep it hot, loaded onto a resupply helicopter, and flown for up to an hour to reach a firing position.

Once, the men were promised steak. After eating C's for weeks, they were eagerly awaiting the arrival of their steak dinners. When the helicopter landed, all the supplies and about a dozen Mermite cans were unloaded. Then the helicopter lifted off. The men raced over, opened the cans, and found liver instead of steak.

The rear-area motherfuckers had kept the steaks and substituted the liver. Immediately, my father got on his radio and called the helicopter flight commander and said, "If you ever bring liver out again, I'm going to shoot you down—and I'm not kidding!"

Once the battalion commander found out that the rear-area people had kept the steaks for a party and sent the liver, he raised holy hell to make sure nothing like that ever happened again.

Arrival

Walking A&P

Wilson and local cadre

Virgil, radio operator

Sgt. Richard Cromartie, tent mate

C-ration delivery

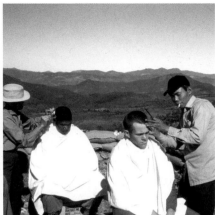

One of six guns in the battery

Ready for liftoff

Thanksgiving with General William Westmoreland

Christmas on the runway in Kontum

Popcorn and rice kettle

North Vietnamese AK-47 and Chicom grenades

Montagnard crossbow

Bronze Star with V for valor

Chuted up for a practice jump

Tho, Duc, and Huyhn

THANKSGIVING

General William Westmoreland, the commander of all U.S. forces during the Vietnam War, had previously been the commander of the 101st Airborne Division. He made several trips out to field locations while my father was in Vietnam. For Thanksgiving in 1966, my father's battalion was in a field position and was going to be served a full Thanksgiving meal—turkey, dressing, mashed potatoes, cranberry relish, and pumpkin pie. In preparation, the men made tables and benches from ammo boxes.

On Thanksgiving, the dinner was prepared in the rear area and flown out to them. To the battery's surprise, General Westmoreland and the author John Steinbeck showed up. Steinbeck was doing research for a book he was writing. Unfortunately, Steinbeck passed away in 1968 before the book was published.

OLD MAN

My father was considered an old man at twenty-five with a wife
and two children. Men would come to him for advice about marital
and girlfriend problems, about being afraid, about what they would
do with their lives when they got back home. Many of the young
men actually had more military experience than my father, but they
needed a father figure.

Toward the end of his tour, his unit had to make a training parachute
jump in preparation for a planned combat jump. My father was
responsible for organizing all the pre-jump training. A couple days into
training, the battery commander's driver came to my father and said,
"Sir, I'm really afraid. I've only got nineteen jumps and haven't jumped
for more than a year."

My father said, "Don't worry, son, it'll all come back. It's just like
riding a bicycle, you never forget once you learn." At this time, my
father only had five jumps and hadn't jumped for more than two years
and couldn't even remember how to chute up.

My father's recon sergeant met a girl on R&R in Bangkok. She was a
prostitute, and he had been sending her money. He said he really loved
her but wasn't sure if she was waiting for him; what did my father think
he should do?

My father had to carefully craft his answer so as not to make the soldier
feel stupid, so he said, "Well, I would be surprised if she was just sitting
around waiting for you to come back. I'm sure she really appreciates the
money you send her. You might want to think about whether this girl
would be the right girl for you to spend the rest of your life with." The
recon sergeant listened and decided that my father had a point. He said,
"You're probably right, what I'm doing doesn't make any sense."

GARY

Gary was my father's good friend in high school and best friend in college. He was a role model for my father—intelligent, strong, steady, and confident. He was also a star football player and champion wrestler. He and my father played sports together and were usually in the same classes in high school and college. They went pheasant hunting and did all the things young men do together.

Both of the men earned chemical engineering degrees at the University of Nebraska. Gary was the kind of person who could look at a physics or chemical engineering problem and visualize the answer without having to solve all the equations, like my father and everyone else had to do. He was brilliant.

They were also in ROTC together and both entered the military after graduation. Gary was a reserve officer and served two years of active duty in the quartermaster corps. He married his high school sweetheart, like my father had.

Gary was sent to Vietnam a few months after my father. He was assigned to run the army post exchange at Tan Son Nhut Air Base on the outskirts of Saigon. This was the primary military base where almost all soldiers arrived and departed. This PX was like a large Walmart. Soldiers could buy virtually anything there that they could have at home.

The only people who were allowed to carry a weapon on base were the base security forces. No other personnel were armed, meaning neither Gary nor any of his staff were armed, so they were totally dependent on base security forces for protection. During the Tet Offensive in early 1967, bases like Tan Son Nhut were targeted by the NVA and the Viet Cong in massive assaults using mortars, artillery, recoilless rifles, machine guns, small arms, and large attack forces. The night they were hit, the base was caught off guard, and all the unarmed personnel were unable to defend themselves. As a result, they suffered heavy casualties.

Gary never recovered from the trauma of that night and was sent home before his tour was complete. Now it would be called post-traumatic stress disorder (PTSD). This was so unlike Gary. My father thought it would have been much harder to be in a situation like Gary's, unable to defend himself or his men.

HOMECOMING

When my father got home, almost everyone seemed more concerned with football scores than the war. However, my mother cared, and that grounded him.

They talked over every detail of his tour. He was an open book with my mother, and later he told his stories to my brother and sister and me. But the fear that my father would have to serve another tour haunted my mother, long after he came home.

My father felt that the war was harder on her than it was on him. He was in action most of the time, while she had time to think about what would happen if he didn't come home.

SOUPY MAN

My brother was eighteen months old when he watched my father's flight take off. While he was gone, my brother often wrapped a towel around his shoulders and ran through the house like "Soupy Man"— shouting, "My daddy fly up in the air, my daddy fly up in the air."

The flight to Vietnam was my father's first as a passenger, even though he had a pilot's license through the ROTC. He had wanted to fly Mohawks—quiet, high-speed, turboprop reconnaissance aircraft that could fly at treetop level to avoid detection. However, as an army officer, he had to serve a year of ground duty before attending the army's year-long flight training program.

By the end of his first year, he had already realized that he did not want to make the military his career, so he turned down flight school and opted for the artillery instead.

STRANGER

I was six months old when my father left for Vietnam. I began whistling and walking and talking while he was gone and didn't remember him when he came home.

I sat in the backseat of the car and stared down at my chest. My brother chatted with my father in the front seat, until I finally slid over the backrest between them and began chatting, too.

BUSINESSMAN

After my father left the army, he got an MBA and we moved to Ohio, then Connecticut. We lived in a small colonial home in Stamford, and my father worked in New York City. He walked to the commuter train and took it to his office in the Chrysler Building.

When he was busy, he would send my mother on errands, like the time he sent her to get the bindings on a pair of old skis adjusted for a Boy Scout trip with my brother. He'd never skied before and didn't know that the skier had to come in to get the bindings adjusted. The men in the shop thought my mother was a hick. She protested. My father didn't mind doing his own chores after that.

SILENCE

My father wanted to become a businessman because he was sure there wouldn't be any politics in the business world. He thought his work would all be judged on merit. So he'd get into a funk every time he had to deal with politics at the office. When he'd get low, he stopped talking to my mother. It was hard on her.

WORK

Bums slept on the sidewalk near my father's office, and a naked woman hung her laundry and sunned herself on a balcony across the street. His office quickly became such a popular spot that he considered selling popcorn.

My father was clean-cut, but he wasn't uptight. He kept a photo of my brother and me on his desk, showing us covered in mud in a "swimming pool" we dug in the backyard. He worked for a power generation firm, first in research and development, then in marketing and mergers and acquisitions.

He moved to a company in Stamford and worked with dealers who sold photocopiers, faxes, and scanners. When he became president of a German typewriter company, he said to his boss, "Why isn't there spellcheck like Brother has?" His boss said in his thick German accent, "Why would you need spellcheck? We don't make mistakes."

The business was done in a few years. Typewriters had no future except as a novelty, an antique. My father went back to working with dealers who sold photocopiers, faxes, and scanners for the rest of his career.

MONEY

My father didn't come from money, and he worried that he wouldn't have enough even after becoming a vice president and moving to a bigger house with a small lake out back. Would he have enough to take care of our family? Would he have enough to retire? Would he be able to keep his job, or find another when he lost one?

When he worried, he'd become silent and blue, and my mother would lose patience with his moods. It took my father years to learn to let his worries go. Once he began to live with pure, moment-to-moment trust, his relationship with my mother righted and his career took off.

He used to envy people who seemed to get everything without struggle, but he learned that true satisfaction lay in good relationships and work done well. He was still working long after his peers had retired. Everyone thought my father was ten or fifteen years younger than he was. He liked getting up early, doing morning chores, swimming in his Endless Pool, doing the elliptical trainer, talking with my mother over coffee, then heading to the office.

He continually achieved his sales and profit numbers and compensated for weaker areas in the business. He usually got thanked for a strong performance with an impossible budget the following year. But somehow he'd make his targets, again and again. Eventually, he had enough to retire without worry, though he'd stopped worrying years before he knew he'd have enough.

FOLKIE

My mother married my father on her nineteenth birthday. She loved my father because he was calm, gentle, kind, smart, hardworking, and handsome. They were best friends. She quit college to go to work as a computer programmer in the statistics lab at the University of Nebraska while my father completed his undergraduate degree. A couple of years later, my brother was born. She had me a year and a half later. Then my father left for Vietnam. While he was gone, my mother taught herself to play the guitar and learned folk tunes by Pete Seeger and Joan Baez—protest songs of love and peace.

When my mother was pregnant with my sister, she had never been so big, so overdue. She could hardly walk up the stairs. After my sister was born, my mother went into a funk. My father was home, but the war was still going on; and she wondered, What kind of world is this? Then one day she thought, Are you going to let this world destroy you? Who will be there for your children? Who will be there for your husband? She decided right then that she would let the sadness go.

But the war still defined my father and mother as individuals and as a couple; it was always there with them. My sister went to college in Washington, D.C., and on a visit, my parents decided to go to the Vietnam Veterans Memorial. It is a very long wall with more than 58,000 names etched on polished black stone panels. It is along a walkway that slowly descends to a low point in the middle and then ascends again to the finish. As my mother descended past the names of the dead, she said she felt like she was being pulled back into the dread she had lived with during the war. She had to get out of there and wait for my father at the other end.

PLATOON

My mother, my father, and my brother went to see Oliver
Stone's *Platoon* at the movie theater. My mother thought it was an
exaggeration—everything that could go wrong went wrong. It made her
angry. She didn't like fiction; she wanted a true story of war. My father
said that each of the events in the movie probably happened, but not to
one person or one unit. My brother began to cry.

"Was it the movie?" my mother asked.

"Yes," he said.

"Did it make you worry about Dad?"

"Yes," he said.

"Are you sad that he could have died?"

"Yes," he said.

He had just finished college and had never cried about that before.

HAPPY PEOPLE

My father "saw some shit" in Vietnam, in the Central Highlands, along the central coast, and by the Cambodian border. I was a baby then. I have no memory of an innocent time, before I carried his war stories in my head, like a movie I'd seen. These are collective memories, family memories, the quiet truths of war borne by all of us, carried and curated as if our own.

War makes no sense, my father always said when we'd watch the *PBS NewsHour* together to honor the dead. It would end quietly, like the silence of those who can no longer speak. Then it was Vietnam; now it is Afghanistan. But war is all the same. I read about a man who served ten tours in the Middle East. He was wounded on the tenth tour by shrapnel in the head and had to learn to talk again. My father served one tour in Vietnam, one year, but this was an infinite year.

When I saw photos in the *New York Times* about a battalion's deployment to Afghanistan, I was moved by a sad man holding his baby and hugging his wife. As I looked at this man cradling his child, I thought of how my life changed as an infant, how those first six months of innocence were cut short, how Vietnam made me who I am—my desire for adventure; my philosopher's distance; my open-mindedness and compassion; my distrust of smiling; happy people who always give good reports; my desire to make order out of chaos and tell stories. I became a journalist, poet, and memoirist—first telling the story of marrying an Israeli man and our slow unraveling after the Gulf War, and now the story of my father's tour in Vietnam.

I wrote on my couch in my Manhattan apartment with a cherry tree below my window, or at a desk at my writers' colony downtown, or in my head on long walks in Central Park. My mother said, "Are you sure it's a good idea to go digging around in the past?"

I thought about what Rumi said, "The wound is the place where the Light enters you."

ROADMAP

My parents were going to Thailand and Cambodia as a bonus
trip for my father's top dealers—the men and women who'd sold the
most photocopiers, scanners, and faxes. My mother planned a trip to
Vietnam first. My mother, father, and I went to see the places my father
had been—Ho Chi Minh City, Na Trang, Phan Rang, Phan Thiet,
Tuy Hoa, and Kontum. My father had always wanted to go back in
peacetime.

We traveled along the coast and up to the Central Highlands, but
we didn't make it to the Cambodian border. We drove north, instead,
toward the border of Laos. The forest was shorter and thinner than he
remembered. The war had been hard on the trees with clear-cutting for
landing zones and batteries, dropping conventional and napalm bombs,
and spraying Agent Orange and other chemicals to strip the foliage and
steal cover.

Logging shrank the jungle after the war, and illegal logging went on
despite a 1997 ban in protected areas. Coffee, tea, rubber, and cassava
plantations broke up the landscape, along with rice paddies where men
and women in conical hats worked in the hot sun. The water buffalo was
their work horse.

My mother copied my father's letters and collected them in a big,
white binder. I had never read them before. He rarely missed days.
Sometimes he wrote more than once a day, always recording the date,
location, and weather. The letters were a roadmap.

My father often mentioned skirmishes and battles, but after Wilson's
death, he no longer talked much about the war. He talked about food
like other men talked about women. He talked about his plans for
graduate school. He talked about where he wanted to live when he got

out of the army. He talked about how he thought about my mother and brother and me when he'd look up at the stars.

I watched his slides, too. I'd seen them many times and knew the stories, but now I was taking notes, asking questions. He was a commissioned officer with the 101st Airborne, the Screaming Eagles, which parachuted into battles during World War II. He began his tour as a first lieutenant and finished as a captain.

When he came home, he didn't have nightmares. He didn't lose sleep, besides abruptly sitting up in bed in the middle of the night to listen for incoming fire, unexpected silence. Even that only lasted a year. Sometimes, my father's mood would get low because of his work as a corporate executive, but he didn't brood about the war. He was a calm, gentle man.

TUY HOA

People rode bicycles and motor scooters; peddled jackfruit, papaya, durian, and nuoc mam—Vietnamese fish sauce—at shop-houses along the roadside; and sold coconut milk, coffee, and tea from aluminum carts, like the young woman across from our hotel in Tuy Hoa. She brewed espresso in the rain for my father and me and brought us small glasses of coffee, thick with sugar.

We stayed in government hotels after moving north to Tuy Hoa, along the central coast. It had been base camp for my father as he patrolled rice paddies and jungle trails. The Tuy Hoa hotel was a big, institutional concrete slab, like a grim Soviet-era place. We were about the only guests.

I had a room with two twin beds. The blanket was old, ratty, and smelled of dog. I began to itch. It didn't feel like dry skin. I tried to put it out of my mind. But the itching persisted.

Fleas? I turned on the light and noticed tiny spots of dried blood on the blankets. Bed bugs? I got up and knocked on my parents' door, telling them, "I can't sleep, I'm itching, I think it might be bed bugs."

I slept in one of the twin beds in my parents' room, and the two of them slept in the other. In the morning, my parents asked for another room. They gave me theirs and took the new one. It had mosquitoes, so they slept under a net.

DUC

After Tuy Hoa, we drove to the Don Xuan market, the place my father bought the pot he cooked rice in. It hadn't changed, my father said. A big tree in the center was a canopy over the market.

Men and women gathered around my father. The women giggled and said he looked good. A man came up to him and quietly said he had served in the South Vietnamese army. He smiled as he spoke to my father, like a friend.

Duc, our driver, maneuvered the minivan through potholes, rocks, and streams to find the spot where Wilson was killed. It was along the Song Ba River, in a valley between ridges, near the Dong Tre Special Forces camp that had become a military base. My father spotted a clearing surrounded by elephant grass, tall as a man. He said it looked like the right place.

Duc was a helicopter mechanic in the South Vietnamese army during the war. He had blue eyes and talked very little. He had come to the U.S. for training at an army post outside of Washington, D.C. He was a cool guy who got along well with my father.

THO

Our main guide, Tho, was an encyclopedia. "Vietnamese history is simple," he said. "We fought the Chinese for a thousand years, the French for ten, and the Americans for twenty." Communism only lasted a decade, Tho said, and now "one communist is one capitalist." I didn't understand what he meant at first, but it became clear as I saw large, modern, oceanside homes and government-owned coffee, tea, and rubber plantations.

Tho and his childhood girlfriend were top of their class. She wanted to marry after high school, Tho said. But he wanted to wait, so she married someone else. He did, too. He showed us a video of his wife and daughter on his cell phone. She was in high school when they met, while he was giving tours of Vietnam. She made sure they stayed in touch.

Tho reminded my mother of Chu. She met him in a computer programming class at a Connecticut community college. He was from Phan Thiet, where my father had gone for almost two days without drinking water in the red sand dunes by the South China Sea. Chu was impressed that my mother knew about Phan Thiet and its fish sauce, nuoc mam. My father used to call it nuke bomb. The smell of fermented anchovies assaulted my father whenever dainty schoolgirls in long, flowing ao dais opened their lunch boxes.

Tho's mother was from Phan Thiet, and his father was a businessman from Hainan, China, who liked gambling and girlfriends and going after the good life. After the war, he was sent to reeducation camp. He practiced Chinese medicine when he got out, but he chainsmoked and died young. Tho would gulp as he told us these things.

Tho had been born after the war, and by the time he went to the university, schools no longer barred people who had been on the wrong side of the war. His older siblings, a brother and a sister, had been excluded, but Tho had a degree in economics and political science.

In Ho Chi Minh City, I bought a bootleg copy of Denise Chong's book, *The Girl in the Picture*, and read that half of the score on the university entrance exam had been political. People with bad profiles had no chance of passing. Even people with neutral profiles could hardly get into a university, like Kim Phuc—the girl shown in a war photographer's famous picture running naked after a napalm bomb burned her clothes and skin.

HUYNH AND AN

Tho told us at breakfast that Hyunh and An were Viet Cong, because of their ages and degrees. Huynh was our local government-provided guide in Kontum. His friend An owned a café.

They had gone to the University of Hanoi to study art. Huynh was a sculptor; An, a painter. Huynh joked that he dropped out because he was hungry and weak. The school only served tapioca, he said. An stayed but could not paint what he wanted—nudes.

Huynh's father built the Bahnar village, where the popular singer Siu Black had grown up. His signature woodwork spanned balconies like sunrays. He was in his nineties and lived near Siu Black's sister, who came to her balcony and flirted with Tho.

I thought of Tho's father, his cigarette habit, his early death. Health, wealth, opportunity—that's how you knew what side people were on. I read this in David Lamb's memoir, *Vietnam, Now*. He had been a war correspondent who returned to Hanoi in peacetime. Tho had been his guide.

RABBITS' BLOOD AND HAPPY ROOMS

One evening, Huynh took us to a small restaurant. Rabbit was on the menu, so we ordered it. As we waited for our meal, we noticed men at the next table drinking bright red liquid out of little shot glasses.

When our waiter brought us our food, we asked him what the men were drinking. He said, "Rabbit blood." After we ate our rabbit dinner, my mother and I went to the restroom. Tho called it the "happy room." It was out back, through a little courtyard, and home to several bunnies.

On our way to the happy room at another restaurant, we passed several women sitting on the ground, washing large chickens in dishpans of milky water. A few feet away was a row of stalls, each equipped with a bucket of water and a dipper. Each happy room had a hole in the back wall that lead to the ground for flushing the stall after it was used.

SORROW OF WAR

Huynh took us to an airstrip in Polei Kleng, in the Central Highlands near Kontum. My father had been there at the end of his tour. The dirt was dry and reddish-tan, like the dirt in Oklahoma where I was born.

He was a boy when my father was in Vietnam. He used to sit by the airstrip in Kontum and watch artillery fire. He said the Americans fired during the day, the North Vietnamese at night.

Huynh led us down a dirt path to a clearing where we could see Chu Mom Ray Mountain. The Americans called it Big Momma. Thousands had died in battles on that ridge. Huynh showed us a haphazard cluster of craters. "Foxholes," he said.

"Are these really foxholes?" my mother asked. She thought people had been digging for scrap metal, leftovers from the war.

The pits looked like egg cartons, bent out of shape. They were random and careless, not the orderly pits I imagined around the battery, sheltering soldiers who took turns guarding the perimeter. Later on, I checked the dictionary: "Foxhole: a pit dug hastily for individual cover from enemy fire."

Huynh climbed into one of the foxholes and picked up an unexploded shell from a 20-millimeter cannon. It looked like a tiny missile, so small he could cup it in his palm. These shells were fired from C-47 cargo planes that soldiers called Puff the Magic Dragon. My mother's father flew C-47s during World War II, when the cargo planes were called Dakotas and Gooney Birds.

Huynh found a few flechettes in another foxhole. They were small as finishing nails and looked like darts—a sharp nose and fins at the tail. This was the sort of antipersonnel round my father had fired at the

NVA when Wilson was killed.

"War is a bad thing," my mother said to Huynh.

He nodded. "Do you know *The Sorrow of War?*"

"Bao Ninh," I said.

His eyes lit up. "Have you read it?"

"Not yet, but I will."

I bought a bootleg copy in Ho Chi Minh City and read it on the plane home to New York. It is a slim, poetic novel about a North Vietnamese soldier haunted by the war and its sorrows.

BUG SPRAY

I skipped lunch, went back to the hotel, and took a shower. The water was cold in the government-run hotel. I bent over and began to cry.

I lay down on the bed in the air-conditioned room. It felt good to be clean of bug spray. We had been wearing it since we left Ho Chi Minh City.

Mornings, I'd stand naked and my mother would spray me up and down because she was afraid of malaria. She'd even spray my hair. It looked greasy, like I hadn't washed it in weeks.

She had two kinds—hybrid Deet and hundred-percent Deet. The first made me so sick that I could hardly function. I slumped over on the seat of the van, sipping sweet drinks. Iced tea, Coca-Cola. The sugar relieved the nausea for a moment. Then I'd sip again. When I switched to hundred-percent Deet, the nausea went away, but an unusual amount of hair began to fall out in the shower.

My mother brought me steak and fries that she'd packed in a baggie. I could not eat.

"I don't want to go out this afternoon."

"Are you sure?" my mother said.

"I'm sure."

After she left, I read Neil Sheehan's *A Bright Shining Lie*, a biography of John Paul Vann. He was an American advisor to the South Vietnamese army, who died in a helicopter crash after the Battle of Kontum. I was near the beginning. What am I doing? I could read this anywhere, the plane, New York. Anywhere. I went to my parents' room and said, "I changed my mind, I want to go out."

We went to the church, the crèche, and the airstrip with peeled cassava where Huynh used to watch artillery like fireworks, then An's garden café.

EVACAFÉ

Evacafé was lush and tropical, like the resort hotels along the shore. The garden had avant-garde sculptures rendered from missiles and scrap-metal remains. A poem by an American veteran hung on a tree. I watched my father and Huynh. They sat next to each other on a bench.

"I feel for people in war," An said. He touched the collar of his shirt, as if touching his heart.

My mother nodded. "Yes, it's very bad."

An looked at me. "What do you do?"

"I'm a writer," I said.

"A writer, for how long?"

"Twenty years."

He smiled.

"Mostly we have soldiers who want to come back," Huynh said. "I had a woman who lost her fiancé in the war."

She brought a photo of him. Huynh held his lighter to the photo, but it wouldn't burn. He noticed her tears, dripping onto the photo. "I wrote a poem on paper and burned it," he said.

"What did it say?" I asked.

"I don't remember. We left it there, in the foxhole."

"Did she ever marry?"

"Yes, she married, but she never forgot her fiancé."

I felt a tear but held it back.

About the Author

Karol Nielsen is the author of the memoir *Black Elephants* and the poetry chapbook *This Woman I Thought I'd Be*. Her work has come out in the anthology *The Moment: Wild, Poignant, Life-changing Stories from 125 Writers and Artists Famous & Obscure* and elsewhere. Her memoir was selected as a New and Noteworthy Book by *Poets & Writers* in 2011 and shortlisted for the William Saroyan International Prize for Writing in nonfiction in 2012. Excerpts were honored as notable essays in *The Best American Essays* in 2010 and 2005. As a journalist, she covered Latin America, the Middle East, New York City, and other beats, contributing to *Jane's Intelligence Review, New York Newsday,* the *Stamford Advocate,* and other publications. She has taught memoir writing at New York Writers Workshop and New York University.

Acknowledgments

I would like to thank the Writers Room for providing an inspiring place to work; Loren Kleinman and Dale Maharidge for writing moving blurbs; Lorna Partington Walsh for her careful copyediting; Maria Abrams, Kristin Perry, and Rachel Sutton at Mascot Books for shepherding the manuscript through publication; Ellen Mitchell, the editor-in-chief of *Jelly Bucket,* and Larry Smith, the editor of the anthology *The Moment: Wild, Poignant, Life-changing Stories from 125 Writers and Artists Famous & Obscure* (Harper Perennial, 2012), for publishing excerpts from this memoir; and my mother and father for their tireless help with this book. I could not have done it without them.

Have a book idea?
Contact us at:

info@mascotbooks.com | www.mascotbooks.com